Money and Finance Guide

Building a Budget and Savings Plan

Terri Dougherty

ReferencePoint Press

San Diego, CA

© 2021 ReferencePoint Press, Inc.
Printed in the United States

For more information, contact:
ReferencePoint Press, Inc.
PO Box 27779
San Diego, CA 92198
www.ReferencePointPress.com

LIBRARY OF CONGRESS CATALOGING-IN-PUBLICATION DATA

Names: Dougherty, Terri, author.
Title: Building a budget and savings plan / by Terri Dougherty.
Description: San Diego, CA : ReferencePoint Press, Inc., 2021. | Series:
  Money and finance guide | Includes bibliographical references and index.
Identifiers: LCCN 2020033646 | ISBN 9781678200480 (library binding) | ISBN
  9781678200497 (ebook)
Subjects: LCSH: Finance, Personal--Juvenile literature. | Budgets,
  Personal--Juvenile literature. | Saving and investment--Juvenile
  literature.
Classification: LCC HG179 .D674 2021 | DDC 332.024--dc23
LC record available at https://lccn.loc.gov/2020033646

Contents

The Freedom of Budgeting

Money, and deciding what to do with it, can be frustrating or exciting. Perhaps you've experienced the disappointment of not being able to afford something everyone else seems to have, whether it's the latest phone, video game, or trendy pair of shoes. Maybe things are heading in the other direction. You just got your first paycheck and can't wait to spend it. Having the power to decide where those dollars will go is a fantastic feeling. Then again, maybe you hate being told that saving, not spending, is the best thing to do with your hard-earned cash. And it's also possible that money just isn't something you want to think about right now. You might wonder why you should be concerned about money when all it seems to do is bring more problems into a person's life.

Becky Smith understands your feelings. As a credit counselor, she helps people sort through financial issues every day. She's helped people figure out how to find the money for next month's rent, build savings, start an emergency fund, and understand what to do when money is being taken out of their paycheck to repay debt they've tried to ignore. She's also bounced back from financial setbacks herself. "Our family had some years where unemployment happened regularly," she explains. "The first time it happened we had no savings, and that's hard. But the next time it happened we were smarter and had some savings. It never dawns on you that a company might go out of business, or you might get laid off for two months. But we experienced that and had to recover."[1]

Like many of the clients she's counseled, Smith had to learn to build an emergency fund and stick to a budget. While she's become an expert at creating a budget, one thing she quickly learned is to be careful when using that word. Although each person's situation is different, when it comes to the word *budget*, they all have one thing in common: none react positively. "They think of restrictions," she says "They think of it as someone telling me what I'm going to do with my money. They see it as limiting."[2]

Creating a plan with a credit counselor early in life can help you avoid major financial issues in the future.

The Freedom to Spend

Far from putting a vise on your ability to spend, a budget can actually provide freedom. Rather than restricting spending, it gives a person the power to decide where money goes. "You might honestly have the freedom to buy what you want and not feel guilty about it," notes Smith, who worked as a financial counselor with Goodwill Industries of North Central Wisconsin. "You have control of your money. You can make it behave. You now have a plan for how you are going to spend your money."[3]

Smith doesn't really like the word *budget* herself, preferring to call it a spending plan. And doing something as simple as giving a budget a more pleasant name can make it easier to create one. That's because budgeting successfully is about much more than working with numbers. It's about being aware of your attitude toward money and understanding your spending habits. It involves adapting, pivoting, and making changes based on the circumstances. If budgeting or creating a spending plan seems like a foreign concept, rest assured that you do have the tools to do it well. You may not know it, but you've already been building the skills you'll need to create an effective spending plan. You can use them to take care of your money and bring security to your financial future.

Chapter One

Where Do I Start?

The thought of creating a budget and saving money can be intimidating. You might envision putting together a massive spreadsheet or creating a complex grid filled with numbers. Being successful at budgeting and saving doesn't depend on an ability to get columns to add up, however. It involves understanding your attitude toward money and how this impacts your spending habits. When you learn to budget and save, you build on skills you already have, like problem solving, patience, and discipline. Learning to budget and save is a step-by-step process that will take your financial habits in the right direction. The important thing is to take that first step by learning more.

It's likely that you've already had a taste of what it's like to budget and save. Mily, age seventeen, has a part-time job at a retail store. When she gets a check, her money goes toward gas and her phone bill first. She'd like to save more, but prioritizing spending is a good first step. She's already putting some budgeting concepts into practice. She can build on those good habits.

Maybe you don't have a job, but it's likely that at some point in your life you've received money for a birthday present or holiday gift. Rather than spending all of it, maybe you've saved to buy shoes, a phone, or a video game. The process of saving toward a purchase or for spending money on a vacation can propel you toward greater savings success in the future. When Emma, age fourteen, was younger, she saved money from her allowance, birthday gifts, and lemon-ade stand earnings in a jar to prepare for a trip to the American Girl Store in Chicago. Before leaving, she counted her money so she knew how much she could spend. She did the same thing when her family planned a trip to Disney World. This simple system helped her become very familiar with the concept of saving money and spending within a budgeted amount.

> "Once a person of any age has that first experience of saving for something they want, and has that satisfaction of saving and buying, that positive experience makes it easier to save for future things."[4]
>
> —Becky Smith, financial counselor

Being careful with how you spend your money, no matter how much you have, and waiting to spend it so you can buy something in the future are good habits. Continuing to practice them can make it easier for you to create a budget and save for larger purchases once you have more money coming in. "Once a person of any age has that first experience of saving for something they want, and have that satisfaction of saving and buying, that positive experience makes it easier to save for future things,"[4] notes financial counselor Becky Smith.

Problem Solving

When you create a budget or spending plan, you're figuring out how to avoid spending more money than you have. This involves problem solving, a skill you've been working on your whole life.

Just as you've learned everything from the alphabet to navigating social media, you can learn how to create a workable budget and save for the future. When you were very young, you couldn't ask someone to help you tie your shoe when you were in the middle of a game on the playground. To solve this problem, you had to learn to tie your shoes yourself. This involved practicing, making mistakes, and trying again until you succeeded.

When you create a budget, you're putting basic problem-solving skills to use. You're looking at what you need to do, how

to do it, and how to take action and improve on what you've done. Just as you didn't tie your shoes correctly the first time, your first budget will contain some mistakes. But no matter how many mistakes you make, you'll be further ahead than if you had never budgeted at all.

Learning and Persevering

We're not born knowing how to manage money. As with mastering other skills, you can learn some tricks and tips that make it easier. You might not know all the ins and outs of budgeting and saving yet, but you do know how to find the information you need. You might learn from your parents or look for information in the library or online. You might learn about it in a class, like seventeen-year-old Morgan, who took a high school class in personal financial management. "I want to look back and say, 'Wow, I made good choices,'"[5] he says.

"I want to look back and say, 'Wow, I made good choices.'"[5]

—Morgan, age seventeen

9

Advice from Mom and Dad

Money might not be an easy topic to bring up with your parents, but you might be surprised by the insights they have to offer. Sara, age eighteen, works at a fast-food restaurant. She puts half of every paycheck into her savings account. She also makes sure she has a fixed amount in her checking account (a fee is charged on some checking accounts if the balance gets too low). Where did she learn these good habits? From her family. "My mom taught me how to budget," she says. "We talk about saving and where I should be spending my money." Sara feels comfortable talking about saving, budgeting, and the topic of money, noting, "A lot of people save money differently so it's nice to get good ideas."

Quoted in author questionnaire, "Building a Budget and Saving Money Survey," March 16, 2020.

Your parents can be a great first step in creating a budget; they have years of experience managing their own money. They may be able to help you avoid mistakes.

Resourcefulness is another skill you likely use often that will help you keep your financial life on track. When you want something that's not readily available, you need to think of another way to reach that goal. If you want to get to the mall to buy a new hoodie but don't have a car, you can use the bus or subway to get there. Maybe you talk to some friends about going with you and split the cost of a ride-share service. Or perhaps you decide that you don't need to go to the mall after all because you've found what you wanted to buy online. By being resourceful, you think of new ways to reach a goal.

Your resourcefulness can help you reach financial goals. These goals can involve saving for college, a car, or a new phone. You probably won't reach your financial goals right away, and that's where perseverance comes in. It's the ability to keep trying and overcome setbacks in order to succeed.

Think about a time you wanted to reach a goal and persevered until you got there. Did you want to learn to play a certain song on the piano, juggle a soccer ball, or create a website? Maybe just open a jar with a really tight lid? You kept trying until you got it. Recalling your past successes can help you keep going when you need to get over a rough patch as you're learning something new.

Practice, Patience, and Discipline

Developing a skill requires both patience and practice. You're not going to paint a masterpiece the first time you pick up a brush. If you're patient, however, you'll improve as you put time into developing your skill. Practice is also part of managing money. You're not going to get it right the first time, but you'll get better at it over time. "Practice makes perfect, which is really old school, but if you feel like your budget didn't work this month it's just implementing tools and changing habits,"[6] Smith says.

Sticking with something involves discipline, and that's another asset that helps you learn something new. The same discipline you apply in other areas of your life can help you succeed

Discipline applies to many things, not just health and fitness. Discipline can also help you stay on the right track to achieve your financial goals.

financially. Do you get up early in the summer to lift weights so you're ready for football season? Do you make ten free throws before you leave the gym? Do you write in your journal every night? You've disciplined yourself to do something that will improve your skills. This discipline can carry over to the decisions you make with money. Before making a purchase, for example, you can discipline yourself to ask questions like, "Will I still want this tomorrow?"

Self-Awareness About Money

Maybe you're not excited about creating new financial habits or refining a budget through practice. When you think about who has money and who doesn't, the concept of money might seem unfair. You might feel like Logan, a seventeen-year-old high school student, who says, "Money is a resource, but not everyone has the same opportunities to access it."[7] Perhaps you think of money as an unpredictable but inescapable part of life, like Grant, age seventeen. Money is "volatile, but it makes the world go 'round,"[8] he says.

Everyone has an attitude toward money, and it's shaped by many different things. It involves your family, your culture, and your age. The environment you grow up in is going to impact the way you feel about finances.

Studies have found that parents play a big role in how a child feels about saving and debt. This is true no matter how much money a family has. Feelings about money are often developed in childhood and are passed down from one generation to the next.

Attitudes toward money are also influenced by environment and culture. These are the customs and values you've grown up with that are practiced by people around you. Lauren Greenfield, author of the book *Generation Wealth*, says that Americans often respect people who are wealthy because they think they could be wealthy one day themselves. "Unlike some other cultures that resent the rich or resent the upper class, Americans admire wealth,"[9] she says.

Varied Attitudes Toward Money

Where you live can shape your attitude toward borrowing and money in general. For example, studies have found the following characteristics in different nations:

- Almost half of Dutch families have taken out loans for things such as cars and homes.
- Only about 10 percent of Italian families have car and home loans.
- People in Austria have less debt than people in the Netherlands.
- People in the German-speaking area of Switzerland are more likely to save money than people in the French-speaking area.
- Americans often believe more money will make things better.

Attitudes toward money are also shaped by age. For example, a young person is more likely to want to avoid thinking about financial issues. This could lead to decisions that quickly have a negative impact on finances, such as spending money without thinking through the consequences. Eventually, overspending could lead to debt and a lower level of confidence in managing money. Being aware of the consequences of avoiding financial issues can show why the topic of money isn't one to brush aside.

It helps to understand that everyone has feelings about money and that such feelings impact the way you use and manage it. This can help you see why you might be likely to make an impulse buy or be reluctant to save. Understanding this can help you make smarter choices and reach your goals.

You Can Master This!

A person's attitude toward money can impact saving, spending, and budgeting habits. Maybe you're one of the many people who cringe at the word *budget* or would rather not think about money right now. However, you likely also understand that one day you'll need to have enough money for food, a place to live, something to wear, and a means of getting where you need to go.

Learning to create a budget or spending plan is well within your abilities. You're already practicing the skills it takes to learn something new, including problem solving, perseverance, and discipline. You've used these skills to master many new tools. A smartphone is a tool that helps you connect with others. A laptop is a tool that brings in information. A workout is a tool that helps improve your fitness level. Learning to budget will equip you with a tool that helps you spend money wisely. Focusing your skills on money management and saving will put you in a better position to have a future that's financially secure.

Chapter Two

Building a Budget

A budget is your plan for spending money, but it's about more than paying bills. A budget puts you in charge of your finances, gives you control over your spending, and helps you reach savings goals. Creating a spending plan lets you make choices that help you worry less and enjoy life.

As twenty-six-year-old Rachel found, it can also keep you from making spending mistakes. Rachel, a structural engineer, was eager to furnish her first apartment. She saw a couch she thought was cute and didn't really think about how much it cost. "I paid a lot for it because I didn't know how much couches were supposed to cost. I literally bought the first cute one I saw online," she says. "Then it ended up being really uncomfortable, and was too short for me to even lie down on." When she moved into an apartment that already had a couch, she sold the couch for half price. Her lesson? A budget can help you think twice before making a costly purchase you regret. "If you don't research and don't think about it first, it's surprising how easy it is to spend money,"[10] she says.

> "If you don't research and don't think about it first, it's surprising how easy it is to spend money."[10]
>
> —Rachel, age twenty-six

A budget gives you the opportunity to think through purchases and manage your finances. It also helps you do the following:

- avoid credit card debt
- save for things you want
- prepare for emergencies
- ease financial uncertainty
- take away guilt over spending money

As Rachel found, planning your purchases helps you make decisions you're happy with. Making the effort to create a budget pays off with better spending habits and peace of mind.

Looking at Income

Before creating a spending plan like Rachel now has, you need to look at how much money you have coming in and where it's currently being spent. This gives you the foundation for creating a budget and deciding where you want your money to go.

You might think that you don't need to learn about budgeting right now because you don't have a lot of money coming in. However, it's never too soon to get insight into good financial habits. Budgeting now allows you to practice money management. You'll gain experience you can build on as your income grows. Sure, you might make mistakes, but they'll be less costly now than if you make them when your income is higher.

Budgeting doesn't hinge on having a certain amount of money to spend. It's about figuring out how to make the best decisions with what you have. For example, Sara, age eighteen, gets most of her income from her job at a fast-food restaurant. Nick, age fifteen, earns income in the summer by mowing his family's lawn. You might get income from an allowance for work you do around the house, gifts for your birthday and holidays, or babysitting for neighbors.

To estimate your income each month, list all the ways you get money. If you have a job, look at the pay stubs to see how

much you bring home with each paycheck. The amount on your check is your net income (the amount you receive after taxes and other deductions are taken out) for that pay period. Most people are paid every two weeks (bimonthly), but a paycheck might also come every week or every month. When adding up your monthly income, include all of the money you get from your job and other sources that month. Multiply that by the number of times you receive it each month to get the total. It might look like this:

Source of income	Amount	Multiply by number of times received each month	Total
Job	$45	2	$90
Babysitting for neighbor	$30	1	$30
Allowance	$10	4	$40
Total monthly income:			**$160**

Why If I Don't Know How Much I'll Make?

If you work at a job where you earn tips, or if your hours at work vary, your income could be different from week to week or month to month. To get an idea of how much you'll be bringing in, look at the average amount you've brought in over the past few months. Use this as a starting point, and adjust your budget if your income changes.

Eric, age twenty-eight, is a self-employed automotive journalist who has been budgeting for a variable income for several years. He's usually paid in the month after his assignments are finished (for example, he's paid in May for assignments he finished in April). He bases his income estimate on the payments he's expecting. He finds it helpful to have a different budget for each month, based on the income he expects and the expenses he's planning for. Eric says:

> "My advice for people who are budgeting with a variable income is to have that written budget unique to each month."[11]
>
> —Eric, age twenty-eight

My advice for people who are budgeting with a variable income is to have that written budget unique to each month and to adjust that income column every time you get a new assignment and can make an accurate estimation of when you'll be paid for it. . . . It might sound hard to predict your income, and it is at first. I learned how to budget mostly by trial and error and it took a few months to really figure out how to do it right.[11]

Track Spending to Find Out Where Your Money Is Going

Eric also breaks down his expected expenses each month, using a spreadsheet to list how much he'll spend on things like insurance, utility bills, and subscriptions. His spreadsheet also has columns for debt (his mortgage payment), savings, and donations. In addition, his spreadsheet includes expenses that are unique to that month. In May, for example, he budgets for gifts for Mother's Day and his son's birthday.

Eric has been budgeting for a while, so he has a good handle on how much he spends each month on various items. To find out where your money is going, track your spending. This lets you

Spending Surprise

No matter how much money you make, the amount you're spending can come as a surprise if you don't keep track of it. The importance of watching spending didn't occur to Mario Fernandez until he lost his job. An oil field rig supervisor in Texas, he was laid off in the spring of 2020 when demand for oil fell as people stayed home to avoid the COVID-19 virus. Workers like Fernandez who had made $100,000 or more a year were laid off. "I didn't realize how much I spent when I was at work," Fernandez told National Public Radio. "Breakfasts. Lunches. Buying my crews food." He wanted to reward his workers for their hard work, but he hadn't realized how much it was costing him. When his income disappeared, he realized how much he had been spending.

Quoted in John Burnett, "Historic Oil Bust Delivers a Gut Punch to a High-Flying Texas County," *Morning Edition,* National Public Radio, May 11, 2020. www.npr.org.

see how all your purchases, big and small, make an impact on how much you spend.

When tracking your spending, it pays to be honest. It might be surprising, or even painful, to see how much money you're spending on certain things. However, you don't need to show your spending tracker to anyone. This is your private account of the money you spend, and you can use it to create a solid budget and improve your spending habits.

One trick Becky Smith suggests is to write down information about every dollar that's spent for two weeks.

That's every single dollar. If you put a dollar in the vending machine, write it down. Now you have a two-week history of how you spend money. Then it might be easier to write your first draft of a budget because you're not guessing as much. Otherwise a person might have a snack budget and say they will spend $10 a week and they spend $40. That's where the tracking comes in.[12]

Track your spending for a few weeks or a month so you capture both purchases you make often and those you only make once in a while. To keep tabs on the details, follow these tips:

- Save receipts for cash purchases. Place paper receipts in an envelope. If there's no receipt, use your cell phone's notes app to make a note of how much was spent or write down the amount in a notebook.
- Check your bank account. Look at the debit card purchases.
- Look at your credit card statement, if you have a credit card. Each purchase will be listed.
- Review monthly bills, such as a cell phone bill or car payment or insurance.

Organize this information by entering it into a spending tracking work sheet. Your spending work sheet might look like this:

Item	Amount
Breakfast sandwich and juice	$5.00
Hamburger and shake	$7.00
Movie	$12.00
Pizza and soda	$12.00
Sparkling water from vending machine	$1.50
New earrings	$15.00
Total:	**$52.50**

Next, sort your spending into categories. They might include the following ones:

- Eating out
- Cell phone
- Clothing
- Personal expenses (haircut, makeup, manicure, jewelry)
- Sports equipment
- Entertainment
- Gas
- Car repairs and insurance
- Savings
- Gifts

Tracking your spending will give you a picture of your spending habits. It can reveal surprises, show you where you can cut back, and help you make better decisions about what to do with your money.

Creating Your Budget

Now that you see where you're spending money, it's time to decide where you want it to go. Your budget will help you spend wisely as it helps you differentiate between things you need to buy and things you want to have. It will also help you increase the amount you save.

A budget gives you the freedom to decide where your money will go. Sure, it ensures that you are setting aside enough money for necessary expenses, but it can also help you find the money for a monthly splurge. For fifteen-year-old Liam, it offers a sense of security. He likes talking about budgeting and saving because he says, "It helps me plan for the future."[13]

A budget is usually created on a monthly basis and is your spending plan for that time period. It's a list of the things you'll spend money on and the amount you plan to spend on them. When you add up all of your spending for the month, it should equal your income for that month. This is called zero-based budgeting because if you subtract your income from your expenses, the answer is zero. It looks like this:

$$\$100 \text{ income}$$
$$- \ \$100 \text{ expenses}$$
$$= \ 0$$

Of course, that's the simplified version. Your budget will contain the details and might look like this:

My income	Amount
Birthday gift	$20
Allowance	$30
Job	$50
Total:	**$100**

My expenses	Amount
Fast food	$20
Cell phone	$30
Gas	$20
Clothes	$20
Entertainment	$10
Total:	**$100**

Expenses of $100 – Income of $100 = 0

What If Things Don't Add Up?

If you add up your expenses and they're more than your income, you have two choices. You can either cut back on spending or bring in more income. The quickest way to balance your budget is to look for places to cut back on spending. Can you eat out fewer times per month? Get a less expensive phone plan? Save on gas by carpooling?

To add more income, you can see whether you could work more hours at your job, do more chores around the house, or pick up some odd jobs from neighbors.

If your income is more than your expenses, the extra money can be used to build savings. This will allow you to afford larger purchases down the road. If you know a big purchase is on the way, set it aside for a specific savings goal. This could be a class trip or new phone, or you could start saving for a larger expense like a new car or college.

Needs and Wants

Once you're on your own, your budget will evolve. You'll be responsible for paying for things like food, a phone, rent, and utilities such as electricity, gas, and water. Your budget will include the cost of transportation, whether that's a car, bike, or bus pass. If you own a home, you'll need to set aside money for taxes, repairs, and general upkeep. These are needs—things you must spend money on.

Today your budget is likely heavy in the wants side. These are things that are nice to have, but you could get along without them. Wants include things like eating out or tickets for movies, concerts, or sporting events. It's really nice to have a new piece of jewelry or take a trip to a water park with your friends, but these are not needs. Wants are your discretionary purchases, and you have more flexibility with how much money you spend on them.

A good rule of thumb is the 50/30/20 rule. You set aside 50 percent of your income for needs, 30 percent for wants, and 20 percent for savings and debt payments. If your income is $1,200 a year, that means setting aside the following amounts:

- $600 for needs
- $360 for wants
- $240 for savings and debt repayment

If you break it down by month, it works out like this:

- $50 for needs
- $30 for wants
- $20 for savings and debt repayment

If you break the categories down further, a budget work sheet might look like this:

Category	Item	Amount
Transportation	Gas	$15
Food	Eating out	$15
Personal items	Phone	$20
	Clothing	$15
Entertainment		$10
Gifts		$5
Savings		$20
Total:		**$100**

Telling the Difference

Sometimes the line between a need and a want is blurry. Do you need a new pair of jeans or do you just want them? Do you need to buy that smoothie at lunch, or could you get by with water? To get an idea of your needs and wants, think about what would happen if you did not buy something. Would your health suffer? Would you lose your job? If something like this would happen, you absolutely need to budget for this item. If the consequences of not buying this are not as dire, the item is a want, and you have more flexibility on how much you spend on it.

It's the Little Things

When seventeen-year-old Morgan looked at his spending, he realized that going on a junk food spree was a big mistake. Like Morgan, you might be surprised by how relatively small purchases add up quickly. You might think you're only buying a few smoothies or burgers, but that can add up to a significant amount over the course of a month or year:

$5 on smoothies x 2 times per week = $10 per week

$10 x 4 weeks = $40 per month

$10 x 52 = $520 per year

If you saved that money, you might use it for one of the following:

- a laptop
- a cell phone
- prom: Dress or tux, ticket, and dinner
- ten meals at a nice restaurant
- five pairs of shoes
- a one-wheel electric skateboard
- a set of skis, boots, and poles

When deciding how much money to set aside for the items in your budget, it helps to rank things by order of importance. This allows you to prioritize your wants in addition to making sure you're setting aside enough money for your needs. Look over the other items listed on your spending tracker and give them a number from 1 to 5. The 5s are things that are most important to you, while 1s are things that you can do without. If you need to cut back your spending or increase your savings, the lower-numbered wants are the place to look. You can list the higher-numbered wants first on your budget and eliminate the lower-numbered wants until your income increases.

One and Done? Nope

A budget is not something you create once and set aside. If you find your spending for the month isn't going as you thought it would, don't throw your budget aside. Do some recalculating. Look for ways to adjust your spending and see what works. Trying again lets you update your plan and fine-tune your spending.

There are many tools you can use to make it easier to update your budget each month. Eric likes to use the free spreadsheet app Google Sheets. "It's very easy to make these columns talk

Making a budget is the best way to see your overall financial picture. It lays out a clear view of your money coming in and going out.

to each other and do the math for you instantly and automatically,"[14] he says. Rachel likes using Excel spreadsheets and can use the program to create graphs that show how her expenses change each month. Emily prefers the Mint app to track her spending and help her stay within her budget's limits. Many other apps—like PocketGuard, Goodbudget, and You Need a Budget—can be used as well. The Federal Trade Commission offers online budgeting tools at www.consumer.gov.

To see what works best for you, give some of these tools a try. You'll benefit from whichever one you choose. Budgeting will help you be more aware of your purchases, spend wisely, and reach your savings goals. You'll probably have to adjust your budget next month, and that's absolutely fine. A budget isn't meant to be a pristine piece of artwork that must be left untouched. It's more like a piece of clay that's easier to handle the more you work with it and is molded into a useful new tool each month.

Chapter Three

Realistic Expectations and Long-Term Goals

In addition to being a plan for how you'll spend your money, a budget helps you save. By dedicating part of your monthly budget to savings, you build toward larger goals. Saving money each month will allow you to realize your dreams, whether that's buying a new sweatshirt or piece of jewelry, taking trip, buying a car, or going to college.

Think about what you want your future to look like. Logan, a high school senior, would love to have a dream car and even an airplane one day. By the time he's thirty, he wants to have his student loans from college paid off. A shorter-term and less expensive goal of his is to buy a book about the role-playing game *Dungeons and Dragons*.

Saving and planning are part of reaching all of those goals. Logan has built a savings account from money he's received for gifts. He'll go to a local public college that's less expensive than a private school, and scholarships will defray some of the cost. He's careful with spending and plans to earn money during summer vacation by doing odd jobs for neighbors. By creating goals and thinking through how he wants to achieve them, Logan has a realistic plan.

Being Motivated to Save

When you're setting money aside, it helps to know what you want to spend it on. You might not want to buy a dream car or airplane like Logan, but you have things you want to do. Maybe you want to go on a date or hang out with friends. Perhaps you'd like to buy new running shoes, a laptop, or a new phone. Maybe you want to travel to London or Jamaica. To get there, you'll need to save.

Having a goal helps you save money because it gives you something important to strive for. If you want to get a good grade on a test, you're motivated to study. If you want to make the team, you practice. A plan to spend time with your friends later gives you an incentive to get chores done now. You can be motivated to save money as well. When you care about a goal, you stick to a plan to reach it. Lauren, age seventeen, saw a pair of shoes she wanted to buy but couldn't afford. She began setting aside money she earned through babysitting so she could make the purchase. "Every time I got money I would take $5 out,"[15] she says. In a month she had enough to buy the shoes.

You might have savings goals like Lauren that you'll reach in a few weeks or months. Maybe you want to go out on a date next weekend, buy something new to wear to the homecoming dance, or go on a class trip at the end of the school year. Recognizing these goals helps you set aside money for them and can keep you from overspending, since you know what your limit is. You might also have medium-term savings goals like a video game system, sports equipment, or a new phone. Setting money aside for these items for a few months or a year lets you make these purchases without going into debt. This saves you even more money in the long run because you're not paying the interest that adds to the cost of a purchase. For example, if you save $500 for a laptop, your purchase costs you $500. If you buy it on a credit card, it will cost you $500 plus a percentage of that amount added every month until you pay it off.

When you motivate yourself to save, you are rewarded for your hard work whether it is a trip with friends, a new TV, or a computer. Saving for your goals pays you back.

Eventually, you'll likely have long-term goals that will take more than five years to reach. They often include savings accounts for retirement and larger purchases such as a car or a home. Building saving habits now will help you set money aside for these larger goals in the future.

How Do You Get There?

So you know that you want to save money, but getting there is another matter. One way to improve the odds that you'll reach your goal is to add some detail to your savings plan. It's not as motivating to have a vague goal like "save money" as it is to put the money toward something specific like "get a new smartphone." Lauren learned this when she was saving for her shoes. She knew what she wanted and how much she had to save to get it. Adding details to your goal helps you know when you've reached it, and that's a great feeling.

When looking at your goal, consider the steps you can take to reach it. Think about what you want to do, how you'll do it, and when you want to achieve it. If you need to save a large amount, break it into smaller pieces by saving for a longer time. Accumulating $500 for a senior class trip might seem daunting, but if you start saving during your junior year, you can reach your goal by setting aside $10 each week.

To create a detailed goal in a concise way, use the acronym SMART. SMART goals are specific, measurable, attainable, relevant, and time-bound. They take what you want to accomplish and put some parameters around it. Here's how a SMART goal breaks down:

Specific: Narrow down what you want to accomplish. Think about exactly what you want to do and what you're saving for. Maybe your specific goal is to save for a vacation, a senior trip, or a car.

Measurable: Estimate how much the item you're saving for is going to cost and decide how much you'll save each week or month. By making a goal measurable, you'll know when it's been met.

Attainable: To make sure this goal is something you can reach, think about how you'll accomplish it. This might mean making changes to your spending habits or finding a way to bring in more money. Maybe to afford formal wear for prom, you'll cut back on eating out or do extra chores around the house every Saturday morning.

Relevant: Think about why this goal is important to you. You're more likely to choose to save money rather than spend it right away when you're saving for something that's meaningful to you.

Time-bound: When do you want to meet this goal? Setting a time frame can motivate you to meet your savings deadline.

A chart like this can help you create your SMART savings goal:

Specific savings goal	I'm saving for:
Measurable	The amount I'll save:
Attainable	To do this I will:
Relevant	This is important because:
Time-bound	I will meet this goal by:

Your SMART goal might read like this:

- I'm going to save $30 so I can go to the movies with Jordan in two weeks. To do this I'll cut back on five fast-food meals over the next two weeks. This is important because we always have a great time together.

- I'm saving $300 by August 1 to buy a new smartphone before going to college. This is important because I need to have a reliable way of staying in touch with family, friends, classmates, and professors. To do this I'll work at a local day care after school and save $15 each week.

Turning a wish or dream into a SMART goal gives you a solid reason for saving money and a concrete plan for doing it. Establishing these parameters helps you avoid getting sidetracked as you make your way toward your goal.

Regulating Spending

Setting a savings goal is a great step, but just setting the goal doesn't mean you've achieved it. You need to stick to the plan. This can be especially challenging when the temptation to spend seems to be all around us. Leah, age seventeen, found herself with some extra time on her hands when the hours at her part-time job were cut back. She filled some of the extra time by going online shopping every day. "It was so easy to scroll and see things I wanted and put them in my cart,"[16] she says.

Leah resisted the purchases by keeping things in her on-line cart and not checking out until the next day, if she bought them at all. Writer Laura Finaldi notes that the temptation to buy doesn't necessarily stop when you click out of the website. In an article about online shopping, she notes that one minute she

In today's society it is easy to spend money online. Teaching yourself to put thought into each purchase takes time, but it is worth every penny.

was admiring a vloggers' lip gloss in a video, and a few clicks later she was on a website where she could buy lipstick and lip gloss for fifty dollars. She didn't make the purchase, but closing the site didn't end the enticement. The website sent her an email a few hours later letting her know that the items were in her shopping bag if she wanted them. "How thoughtful,"[17] she writes.

Making an impulse buy has never been easier. The opportunity to spend money can pop up when you're scrolling through social media or reading an online article. It's easy to add a candy bar to your purchases when the candy is right by the checkout register, or maybe you pick up a quick burger at the drive-through on your way home from school.

These impulse purchases may be more common than you think. One study from online shopping website Slickdeals found that Americans impulsively buy three things each week and spend around $450 a month on impulse buys. That's $5,400 a year and can add up to $324,000 over their lifetime.

Can a Middle Schooler Afford a Laptop?

Buying your own laptop might seem like a tall order for a middle school student, but this one managed to pull it off: "I didn't have a job, but I had saved up money for two or three years," says Logan, now a high school senior. "I was determined to buy a laptop. I wanted to play video games and watch movies." He admits he knew nothing about computers, but his parents both worked in information technology. They suggested he look online to see whether he could find a used laptop that would be less expensive than a new one. "The guy I bought it from was super nice and thought it was cool that I had saved $300," Logan says. "He sold it to me for $250." The computer worked for Logan throughout high school. "It definitely got the job done," he says.

Logan, interview by the author, May 6, 2020.

Do you wonder how much impulse buys cost you? Take a look at your spending tracker. Review debit card and credit card statements and notes you've made about spending in your phone's notes app or in a notebook. Which purchases were impulse buys? The fact that shopping has never been easier means that you need to be more vigilant than ever about where your money is going.

Reining In Impulse Buys

Emotion plays a significant role in impulse spending. Making a purchase can be temporarily exciting, and buying something can make you feel like you're in charge of your money. An impulse buy might seem like an act of freedom; however, when you make an impulse purchase, you're buying what someone else wants you to get, and you're buying it on their timetable. You can free yourself of their influence by not making the purchase. By planning your spending, you're not letting someone else dictate how you spend your money. "I have thought about it in terms of a game," says Kyle, age twenty-eight. "If I choose not to buy something, I'm winning because they haven't tricked me into handing my money over to them."[18]

> "I have thought about it in terms of a game. If I choose not to buy something, I'm winning because they haven't tricked me into handing my money over to them."[18]
>
> —Kyle, age twenty-eight

Asking yourself these questions before you make a purchase can help you cool an impulse to spend:

- Do I need this?
- Will I still want this tomorrow?
- Will I use this?
- Will this make me happy?
- Is this in my budget?

Not every impulse purchase opportunity is the same, and it can be tough to think things through when you're faced with the chance to make a quick buy. Here are twelve additional ways to avoid buying when the urge strikes.

1. **Remember that you have time.** It's no accident that some deals expire quickly or that there are only a few items left in stock. This plays on people's fear that they'll miss out or that others will get to experience something they won't. No matter what the ad says, the deal will come back.

2. **Play the waiting game.** If you see a great deal, don't tell yourself no. Tell yourself you're going to wait. Then sleep on it and see if you feel the same way about the purchase. Leah likes to use a rule she learned in class. "I was taught in personal finance class to wait two weeks, and if I still want it I can buy it then,"[19] she says. A little bit of distance will help take the emotion out of your purchase.

3. **Hold it.** When sisters Emma, age fourteen, and Katie, age twenty-one, see a sweater, shirt, or pair of jeans at the mall that they really want to buy, they put it on hold. Then they go visit a few more stores or get something to eat. The extra time helps them judge whether the item is still a must-buy. "Sometimes when it's right in front of you it seems more important than it really is,"[20] their mom, Kelly, says.

4. **Pay in cash.** The price you pay for something can become more real when you see money leaving your hands. When buying something at a store, pay in cash to be more aware of how much you're spending.

5. **Take a list and set a limit.** Before heading to a store or the mall, make a list of what you want to buy. Estimate how much things will cost and take that amount of cash with you. Red, age eighty-nine, puts it this way: "When you go to town, don't put money in your pocket that you don't intend to spend."[21]

6. **Look at your goals.** Write your savings goal or the amount you want to spend on a piece of paper and wrap it around your debit or credit card. This will remind you of your spending limit for the day and why you don't want to spend too much.

7. **Make checking out harder.** When you shop online, shop as a guest. The need to enter your information each time will give you extra time to think about the purchase. Also, order from a website rather than downloading the app. This reduces the temptation to quickly enter an order from your phone.

8. **Turn off social media.** When ads are constantly showing up on your apps or in your email, it can be hard to resist them. To avoid these marketing messages, try staying away from social media for a set amount of time.

9. **Look for shopping triggers.** Do you buy impulsively when you're hungry? After grades come in? Think about other ways to cope. Make sure you have a healthy snack with you to eat after school so you don't stop at a fast-food restaurant. Plan to talk about your grades with someone rather than heading to the mall to celebrate or try to cheer yourself up.

10. **Change your habits.** If your impulse buys center on fast food, try changing your routine so you're not faced with as many opportunities to buy it. Pack your lunch or a snack rather than buying one. Take a different route home from school or work so you don't go past a fast-food restaurant.

11. **Tell others about your savings goal.** Let others know that you want to go on the class trip or buy a new phone before you start college. They can help you be accountable for saving and can help keep you on track.

12. **Budget for surprises.** If your budget seems too rigid, build in some flexibility. Set aside money to spend on whatever you want that month. You can call it a slush fund or fun money. If a surprise purchase comes up, go ahead and buy it, but stay within your spending limit for the month.

Saving with the Envelope System

To get a feel for how much money you're spending, use the envelope system. To do this, you'll use cash. Here's how the system works:

- Withdraw enough cash to cover your spending for the month.
- Create an envelope for each category in your budget (such as food, entertainment, and clothing).
- Place the amount you have budgeted for that item into the envelope.
- When you need to make a purchase from a category, use money from the envelope.
- If you spend all the money in one envelope before the month ends, don't borrow from other envelopes.
- Save any money that's left at the end of the month.

Seeing cash leave your hands every time you buy something can give you a clear understanding of the amount you're spending.

If you can't stop making impulse buys, think about why you're doing this. Are you trying to be cool? Feel better about yourself? Is there something lacking in your life that you think a purchase will fix? Buying something new won't make problems go away. Consider what's motivating your purchases and think about other ways to boost your self-esteem. When impulsive spending can't be controlled, it can turn into a destructive habit. If your spending is putting you in debt, or you can't seem to ever say no, talk to a teacher, an older sibling, your parents, or a counselor about what you're experiencing. They can help you find ways to cope and turn things around.

How Can I Save When I Don't Have Any Money?

Maybe impulse purchases aren't your problem, but you still can't find a way to save money. A little bit of creativity can make saving more interesting, and best of all, it works. Try these ideas for kick-starting your savings habit:

- **The two-liter trick.** This is a sneaky way to save several hundred dollars. At the end of the day, put your change into a two-liter bottle. By the time it's filled, you could have more than $500 in there.

- **The savings jar.** Emma saves her coins in a glass jar. "I take it to the bank when it's full,"[22] she says.

- **The fifty-two-week challenge.** To take this challenge, you start by saving $1. Each week, you increase the amount you save. (In week 1, you save $1. In week 2, you save $2. In week 52, you save $52.) If you do this for a year, you'll save $1,378. Of course, this gets tougher as the year goes on. But even if you plateau at $5 a week, you've created a savings habit.

A great way to save money is by putting all your extra change into a jar. When it is full, cash it in to add to your savings account. You might be surprised how quickly it fills up.

- **Set a limit.** Lily, age seventeen, has a debit card account that her parents helped her set up. There is $500 in the account, and she uses the money for eating out with friends, buying clothes, and paying for gas. The limit helps her be more aware of her spending. "Once that runs out, that's it,"[23] she says.

- **Pay yourself first.** Lily, who works at a bakery, has her paycheck deposited directly into her savings account rather than to her debit card account. "I don't spend any money from the savings account,"[24] she says.

- **Skip one fast-food meal each week.** Pack a sandwich, fruit, string cheese, and some fresh veggies for lunch instead of heading out for fast food. You'll save money, time, and calories.

- **Look for free fun.** Check out entertainment options at local libraries, museums, and community centers. Watch for free concerts in the park. Take a walk at a local nature center or play tennis on public courts.

- **Be selective with streaming.** The cost of entertainment streaming services can add up quickly. Make a list of all the music, video, and other streaming services you subscribe to and their cost. See how many you can live without. If you cancel and find you really miss it, you can always sign up again.

> "I'm basically saving now so I'm not in debt later in life."[25]
>
> —Cassidy, age eighteen

Getting into the habit of saving now will make it easier to make it a priority in the future. Cassidy, age eighteen, learned the value of saving after a spending spree almost drained her savings account. She now saves at least half of her paycheck from her job at a restaurant and expects this to save her some anxiety down the road. "I save so I can buy a car or house some day with little to no interest and never be worried about bills," she explains. "I'm basically saving now so I'm not in debt later in life."[25]

Chapter Four

How to Find the Sweet Spot

When Emma, age fourteen, needs to learn about being content with money, she looks to her grandfather, Red. He doesn't worry about having the biggest house on the block or the fanciest car. He likes hearing about the vacations his friends take but doesn't envy their travels. He's not tempted to try to make money quickly with an investment scheme. He likes to say that he has something his friends don't have: He has enough.

Knowing when you have enough money is great for peace of mind, but getting there can be tricky. How do you know when to spend your birthday money and when you should save it? How do you know when you should buy that new sweatshirt and when you should walk away? How do you know when your savings account is big enough? Getting saving and spending habits in sync involves both planning and self-awareness. You need to know what you want your money to do for you and what contentment is like.

Can Money Buy Happiness?

One common financial pitfall is thinking that more money always brings more happiness. This isn't true. Buying something doesn't necessarily make you content for long. When Nick, age fifteen, plays video games, he's tempted to buy new outfits, or skins, for his character. He's collected a number of them over the years, including some he now regrets buying. When he's tempted to buy more, he thinks about the ones he no longer uses. "Sometimes when stuff comes out it seems really cool," he says. "But then I think about the other skins I don't really like."[26]

Studies have shown that people are happier, to a point, when they make more money. However, earning more and more money does not necessarily make a person feel content or successful. While people need enough money to cover basic needs like food, clothing, and shelter, having a great deal more to spend on whatever they want doesn't necessarily make people happier. Studies have found that people who make $75,000 to $105,000 a year are most satisfied with their lives. They have enough money to buy what they need and don't have to worry about the negatives that come with having more money.

It might surprise you that earning more money has downfalls. But researchers have found that people don't necessarily want to have more money. What people really desire is to have more money than someone else. Researcher Michael Norton found that people often compare themselves with others when deciding whether they are satisfied with their lives. These comparisons can make even a rich person feel unfulfilled. People with millions of dollars might not feel like they have enough money because they feel they need more money than other people they know. Norton points out that a person who makes $50 million a year might feel unsuccessful if he or she moves into a neighborhood where most people are making more than that.

> "All the way up the income-wealth spectrum, basically everyone says [they'd need] two or three times as much money before they would be perfectly happy."[27]
>
> —Michael Norton, researcher

For his research, Norton and his collaborators asked millionaires how much more money they would need to reach the top of the happiness scale. He told writer Joe Pinsker, "All the way up the income-wealth spectrum, basically everyone says [they'd need] two or three times as much" [27] money before they would be perfectly happy. Norton's research shows that even when you have more than enough money to buy what you need and want, you won't necessarily be happy. Trying to keep up with what others have and always wishing you had just a little bit more can make you miserable.

So, What Does Bring Happiness?
Close relationships, rather than earning more money, make people happier throughout their lives. A Harvard study that followed people for decades found that good relationships kept people happier and healthier. Rather than great wealth, it was social connections and good, warm, close relationships that led to a happier life.

Money can't buy happiness; in fact researchers have found that having good relationships keeps people happier and healthier.

Lily, age seventeen, certainly agrees. The opportunity to see her friends often drives her decision to go out to eat. If going to restaurants isn't your style, Lauren, age seventeen, suggests having some free fun with your friends by going to a local park, hanging out at a friend's house, or playing a game like volleyball in the backyard.

The Power of Giving

Giving gifts to others, in addition to spending time with them, will also boost your happiness level. Emma saves money to buy holiday gifts for friends and family members. "It feels better to buy things for them than for myself," she says. "If you buy clothes for yourself you might feel guilty but when you're buying for other people it feels really nice."[28]

> "When you're buying for other people it feels really nice."[28]
>
> —Emma, age fourteen

Research backs up her positive feelings toward giving. Studies have shown that spending money on others brings happiness. The happy feeling that comes with giving to others might be because giving releases hormones that produce positive feelings. It stimulates areas of the brain associated with pleasure and social connection.

Researchers have found that people do not need to be rich or donate a huge amount of money to be happier. Even small amounts make a difference. "Although people believe that having money leads to happiness, our research suggests that this is only the case if at least some of that money is given to others,"[29] says Norton.

How Much to Give?

To find money in your budget for giving, remember the 50/30/20 rule. Under that rule of thumb, you set aside 50 percent of your income for needs, 30 percent for wants, and 20 percent for savings and debt payments. Some of the money in your "wants" column could be set aside for giving. Perhaps you want to support a charity or church. Maybe you want to set aside a certain amount of

Does More Money Bring More Work?

Making more money can leave you less satisfied with your life, and it might also bring more work. A bigger paycheck can mean that you face

- more demands on your time,
- a higher workload, and
- a loss of time for rest and relaxation.

Researcher Andrew T. Jebb found that earning more money makes people happier only to a certain point, after which it does not improve their well-being. "That might be surprising as what we see on TV and what advertisers tell us we need would indicate that there is no ceiling when it comes to how much money is needed for happiness, but we now see there are some thresholds," he says.

Quoted in Tim Evans, "Money Can't Buy You Love, but What About Happiness? Purdue Research Says Yes, to a Point," IndyStar, February 16, 2018. www.indystar.com.

money each month for gifts for family and friends. Earning money to support and help others can make you happier. You have more time and resources to give to others when you don't worry about having as much yourself.

Making giving part of your budget can help you do it thoughtfully. Now that you know what research says about money, giving, and happiness, you might think that that the answer is to give it all away. While you certainly have the power to do what you want with your money, think about how giving fits into your budget. Just as making an impulse purchase isn't a smart thing to do, impulsively giving money away is not a wise financial decision. When Kyle visited Italy, he participated in the tradition of tossing a coin into Rome's Trevi Fountain. After he tossed a euro coin in, he realized the coin had been worth more than he thought.

Charitable giving should be included in your budget, so set aside money each month for a charity or church of your choice. It not only helps others, it makes you feel good.

While it's rare to actually throw money away, it's never a bad idea to put thought into where your money is going. If you're asked to support a charity you're not familiar with, do some research into the organization to find out whether it uses its funds in a way that you agree with. While giving has been shown to make people happier and is a valid part of a budget, you still need to be able to pay your bills and build savings for the future. Intentionally including giving in your budget lets you enjoy the benefits of giving without jeopardizing your financial security.

Your Beliefs, Your Decisions

A tendency to give money away can actually stem from a person's attitude toward money. Researcher Brad Klontz looked at people's beliefs about money and their financial behavior. He developed four categories into which people's views of money can be put:

- money avoidance
- money worship
- money status
- money vigilance

These views toward money each come with financial pitfalls, and understanding the drawbacks can help a person do a better job of managing money and understand how to find the sweet spot with spending habits. Here are examples from his four categories:

Money avoidance: People may avoid money because they think they don't deserve it or because they see danger in having it. As a result, they may spend unconsciously or give money away. A person who views money as bad is likely to be aged eighteen to thirty, be single, and have a lower income. Avoiding thinking about money or putting off dealing with finances can bring anxiety in the long term. Debt, lower self-esteem, and great stress could all build. To overcome money avoidance, keep track of income and spending and create a spending plan. Try using direct deposit to build your savings account or try a phone app to make it easy to track spending.

Money worship: People who worship money think that all their problems will be solved by a financial windfall or higher income. They can be at risk for overspending, gambling, becoming a workaholic, and compulsive hoarding. They risk getting into debt and are likely not to pay off their credit card each month. To overcome a tendency toward money worship, it is important to understand the role money plays in your life and how it balances with other elements such as family, faith, and health.

Money status: People who value the status money brings are eager to have the things money can buy. They can become too concerned about financial success and be less happy and more anxious. They also could easily fall into debt. Realizing that money won't buy happiness is important to the well-being of people who fall into this category.

Money vigilance: People who are vigilant about money are hesitant to share information about income or wealth. They risk not investing it properly. They may save and live frugally, but too much anxiety can keep them from enjoying the benefits of spending money. On the bright side, people who are vigilant about money also pay off their credit card bill monthly and don't spend foolishly.

Tracking Spending Brings Satisfaction

When it comes to feeling good about your financial situation, knowing where your money is going can have a more significant positive impact than a larger income. Financial coach Maggie Germano says that many people mistakenly think that earning more money will decrease financial stress. "That's actually something that I hear a lot, where they think that if they just increase income, that everything would get better," she says.

However, a bigger paycheck doesn't necessarily ease stress or bring happiness. If your spending goes up when your income does, your savings won't increase. Germano finds that a person can be frustrated by a feeling of "living paycheck to paycheck" even after earnings go up.

Instead, being aware of how your money is being spent can make you feel better about your finances and the purchases you're making. Germano finds that those who feel the best about their financial situation have a clear understanding of what they're spending money on. When her clients look at their purchases, they might be surprised by how much money went toward online shopping, for example. Knowing this can help them channel it toward things that are more fulfilling. Having a positive feeling about your finances "is less about how much is actually coming in and more about how they're consciously using the money," Germano says.

Quoted in Joe Pinsker, "Who Actually Feels Satisfied About Money," *The Atlantic*, July 21, 2019. https://www.theatlantic.com.

When you looked at these categories, you may have felt like bits and pieces of different categories described you. This is normal. People usually fall into more than one category. One attitude may strongly describe them, while pieces of the other attitudes also fit. These views toward money each come with drawbacks, and understanding them can help you do a better job of managing money.

Keeping Things in Balance

Recognizing which attitudes apply to you can help you watch out for choices that can lead to poor money management. Being aware of how your attitude impacts your spending habits allows you to make better decisions regarding your money. When you understand your tendencies, you know what to build on and what to dodge. Leah, age seventeen, knows she has a tendency to want to buy things she doesn't really need, so she listens to her friends when they tell her to be cautious. "They tell me, 'You do not need that,'"[30] she says.

Remember, friends, relationships, and gift giving bring more happiness than having more money. If you tend to worship money or see it as a way to achieve status, you might be tempted to keep trying to earn more and more as you strive for happiness you're never going to achieve. If you avoid money, you might be tempted to give it away without thinking about your bills or saving for an emergency. Remembering the basics of budgeting, and breaking your spending into needs, wants, and savings, can help you prioritize your spending in a way that ensures you have enough to cover your expenses and allows you spend without feeling guilty. Thinking about your attitude toward saving and spending can help you develop good habits, avoid mistakes, and understand when you have enough.

Chapter Five

The Unexpected: Be Ready for an Emergency

Getting to work and school on time was no problem for seventeen-year-old Leah until an accident put her car in the shop. She was without a car for almost a month while she waited for the car to be fixed and then earned money to pay for the repairs. Her parents paid the repair shop for their work on the car, but didn't allow Leah to drive the car until she had earned enough money to pay them back. She did have the option of borrowing her parents' car to get to work, but that didn't always work out. "There was one time when my mom didn't come home from work in time and I was late for work, and that stressed everyone out," she says. "It was not ideal at all."[31]

That experience helped Leah understand how to deal with a financial emergency and the importance of having an emergency fund. When something goes wrong and you're faced with a surprise expense, you need to figure out how you'll pay the bill.

When an Emergency Arises

An emergency fund helps a person withstand an unpleasant financial surprise. This might come in the form of an accident, like Leah experienced. It could also happen if you lose your job or if work you had counted on fails to materialize.

Vinny, age eighteen, had been counting on earning money for college by working at a local swimming pool, but he had to change his plans after the pool he planned to work at was closed. Instead, he took a job mowing lawns for his grandfather's property management company. Lauren, age seventeen, had a similar experience. The summertime babysitting job she had been counting on was canceled when the family she had been working for no longer needed her, so she earned spending money in the summer by mowing her grandfather's lawn. She wasn't earning as much as she had at her babysitting job, but it was something.

Looking Elsewhere

When your income drops or an unexpected expense arises, it can help to have some money set aside to take care of expenses. If you don't have an emergency fund when you're in need of cash in

When an emergency arises it can take a toll on you financially. If you have an emergency fund it will save you from going into debt from the unexpected expense.

a hurry, your options are limited. You'll have to do without, revise your plans, or look elsewhere to get the money you need.

When you're on your own, an unexpected financial shock can have more serious consequences. You'll have to find a way to pay for rent, food, and transportation. A survey by the Federal Reserve Bank found that when people need money but do not have an emergency fund, they respond in the following ways:

- put the expense on a credit card and pay it off over time: 16 percent
- borrow from a friend or family member: 10 percent
- sell something: 6 percent
- use money from a bank loan or line of credit: 3 percent
- use a payday loan, deposit advance, or overdraft: 2 percent
- delay paying for the expense: 12 percent

These options solve a financial problem in the short term but can lead to other issues down the road. For example, using a credit card means that you'll need to figure out how to pay the amount that you have charged to the card, plus interest. When a balance isn't paid off each month, interest can quickly inflate the amount owed. For example, if you owe $1,000 on a credit card with a 16 percent interest rate and make the minimum payment of $40 per month, you'll pay a total of $396.70 in interest, and paying off the debt will take five and a half years. Amy, who now teaches a class in personal finance to high school students, knows that it's easy for anyone to get into debt if they don't have a budget. She had to overcome the credit card debt hurdle when she was in college. "I got into credit card debt and could never figure out how to get out until I budgeted,"[32] she says. In addition, she didn't set aside money in an

> "I got into credit card debt and could never figure out how to get out until I budgeted."[32]
>
> —Amy, high school personal finance teacher

Banking Your Raises

One way to build your emergency fund is to bank your raises. Rather than spending the extra money, send it to your bank account. Larry Bolt of Florence, Oregon, used this method. When he got a raise, he used the money to build up his retirement savings or a similar savings account. "Whenever I received a raise, I pretended I hadn't," he says.

Quoted in *AARP the Magazine*, "Money Magic," April 2020, p. 47.

emergency fund, so she didn't have a financial cushion to rely on for unexpected expenses.

You can ask family and friends to help you pay for an unexpected expense, but asking for financial help can lead to fractured relationships if loans aren't paid back on time. And if the people you are relying on for money are also short on funds, you're out of luck.

If you decide to sell something to make ends meet, you might find that it brings in less money than you thought it would. In addition, once something is gone, it's gone. You won't be able to turn to this source of income in the future.

Making It Work

When things go wrong, you might have to do without something you once depended on, as Leah did with her car. A broken laptop might mean you have to use a computer at school or a local library. If your bike gets a flat tire, you might have to walk or borrow one until it gets repaired.

You can also use some ingenuity to come up with a solution. Lauren's phone didn't work well, but her parents were reluctant to buy her a new one. After it broke, she had to go without one for a week while her parents shopped around for a good deal. Her parents were able to reach her through her friends' phones, but that wouldn't work as a long-term solution. "That was not good for me," she says. To solve the problem, she bargained with her parents and agreed to pay them $30 a month so she could get the phone more quickly. "I kind of needed it because I didn't have a phone, so I was like, I'll pay the $30 a month if you'll get it for me now,"[33] she says.

Creating an Emergency Fund

One way to be ready for a financial setback is to create an emergency fund. An emergency fund is a source of money you can dip into when something goes wrong. You might face a car repair bill like Leah did or need a new phone like Lauren. When emergencies like these arise, having money set aside in a special fund can help you weather the storm.

Creating an emergency fund is one of the best things you can do to help your future self. You never know when an emergency will happen or how much it will cost.

Creating an emergency fund doesn't come naturally to most people, however. In fact, the majority of people struggle to save. A 2018 survey by the Federal Reserve found that four in ten adults would have a difficult time covering an unexpected $400 expense, and a 2019 survey from the Financial Health Network found that less than a third of Americans were financially healthy. While most were confident they could pay their bills on time, most lacked savings they could tap into in case of emergency.

Setting Up an Emergency Fund

With an emergency fund, you have a resource to tap into without going into debt. Emily, age twenty-four, learned the value of an emergency fund when she found herself without a job after a summer internship was canceled. "I usually make enough in the summer to last me through the school year, so when this happened my checking account was low," she says. "I hadn't experienced an emergency issue with money before, but you can't predict life and things are going to happen to you that aren't in your favor. When this happened I was forced to adapt." She spent money on needs, not wants, and when she got another job, she began putting a percentage of her paycheck into a savings account. "I wanted to be prepared for the next situation that might put me into financial despair,"[34] she says.

> "I hadn't experienced an emergency issue with money before, but you can't predict life and things are going to happen to you that aren't in your favor. When this happened I was forced to adapt."[34]
>
> —Emily, age twenty-three

To be prepared for a downturn, people are commonly advised to have enough money to cover three to six months of living expenses. This rainy-day fund can help cover the cost of essentials like food, housing, and transportation. It can also be used to cover a large one-time expense such as a car repair, broken appliance, or new roof. To determine how much to aim for in an emergency fund, follow these tips:

1. Look at the list of expenses in your budget.
2. Find the ones you *need* to spend money on each month.
3. Add up the amount you spend on them.
4. Multiply this total by three (or four, five, or six if you'd like to set aside more).

This is your goal for savings that you can tap into in the event of a surprise expense. You will want to set this up as a separate account so you don't think about spending it.

Funding Your Emergency Fund

Once you see the amount you should have in an emergency fund, you might be tempted to give up. Even when you know that setting aside money in an emergency fund is important, looking at the total you are aiming for can be daunting. It might seem like saving $300 is next to impossible. Becky Smith, a financial counselor, has seen it happen with clients she works with. "That can be a tough pill to swallow," she says. "It can make someone say, 'That's too hard, I'm not going to do it.'"[35]

To get over this hurdle, Smith suggests saving a portion of every paycheck. It doesn't need to be a large amount. "If your money goes into direct deposit, ask your credit union or bank to transfer $20 to savings every time the direct deposit hits,"[36] she says. Having the money automatically transfer to that account lets you build your savings without thinking about it.

> "If your money goes into direct deposit, ask your credit union or bank to transfer $20 to savings every time the direct deposit hits."[36]
>
> —Becky Smith, financial counselor

When Things Don't Go as Planned

Creating an emergency fund and watching it grow brings a feeling of security. When a financial emergency happens, other

Small Expenses May Result in Hardship

A 2019 survey conducted by the U.S. Federal Reserve Bank revealed that relatively small, unexpected expenses can be a hardship for many families without adequate savings. Faced with an expense of $400, most respondents said they would carry a balance on a credit card or borrow from friends or family. Twelve percent of adults said that they would be unable to pay the expense at all.

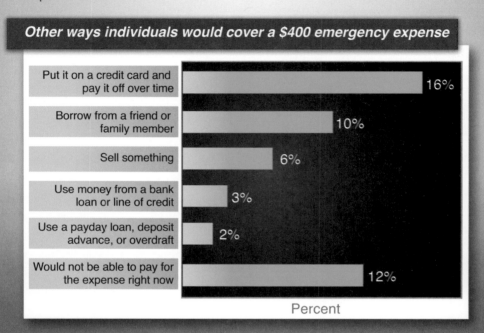

Other ways individuals would cover a $400 emergency expense

Category	Percent
Put it on a credit card and pay it off over time	16%
Borrow from a friend or family member	10%
Sell something	6%
Use money from a bank loan or line of credit	3%
Use a payday loan, deposit advance, or overdraft	2%
Would not be able to pay for the expense right now	12%

Percent

Note: Respondents can select multiple answers.

Source: www.federalreserve.gov.

emotions will be involved. If you get into a car accident, break your phone, or lose your job, you might experience anxiety, frustration, sadness, and anger. These emotions should not be ignored. You can deal with them by talking to family, friends, or a counselor.

Having an emergency fund will make it easier for you to work through the financial side of the situation. It's important to be proactive and take steps to deal with the costs you're facing. Trying to avoid bills or constantly planning to deal with them later will

One Step at a Time

If building a well-stocked emergency fund of several thousand dollars seems daunting, try reaching smaller goals first. For example:

- Step 1: Save one month's rent.
- Step 2: Save $1,000.
- Step 3: Save one month's expenses.

"We are incrementally building this savings," notes financial counselor Becky Smith. "If I tell someone to save one month's rent and they can't do it, I'll tell them to try to put $20 in savings next month." This allows steady progress to be made toward the goal. For example, if your monthly rent is $500, you can reach this goal in about six months if you save $20 per week. If you keep going for the rest of the year, you'll reach step 2 and have $1,000. Then you can aim for step 3.

Becky Smith, interview by the author, March 28, 2020.

only make the problem bigger. Missed payments bring fees and added interest. Do your best to assess your financial situation and come up with a plan.

When an emergency arises, figure out how long your emergency fund will last or how much of the surprise expense it will cover. If it won't cover everything, take action. Ask about payment plan options, turn to family and friends for loans, look for ways to cut back on spending, or bring in cash by selling furniture, a bike, or a car. These solutions are not ideal, but they are better than allowing bills to mount. A financial emergency will involve dealing with change and uncertainty. Taking steps to get the financial side figured out will provide a sense of control and allow you to have more energy to focus on the other aspects of the situation. Once things settle down, learn from the situation and restock your emergency fund.

What's an Emergency?

Thankfully, emergencies are rare. This can bring up another issue, however. Once you have reached your emergency fund goal of several months of expenses, you will have a good deal of money set aside. The question of what justifies spending it will inevitably arise.

A job loss, natural disaster, and car or appliance repair all qualify as emergencies. Other situations are not as clear. To determine whether a situation is an emergency, ask yourself the following questions:

- Is this expense necessary?
- Was this expense unexpected?
- Do I need to buy this right now?
- What will happen if I don't spend this money?

If you answer yes to the first three questions, and the consequences of not spending the money will be dire, the situation is an emergency. You can justify using the money in your emergency fund.

Can Fun Be an Emergency?

You may also have the opportunity to take a trip with a friend and save money by splitting the cost of the travel and hotel. You might come across a great deal on car or a fantastic sale on shoes.

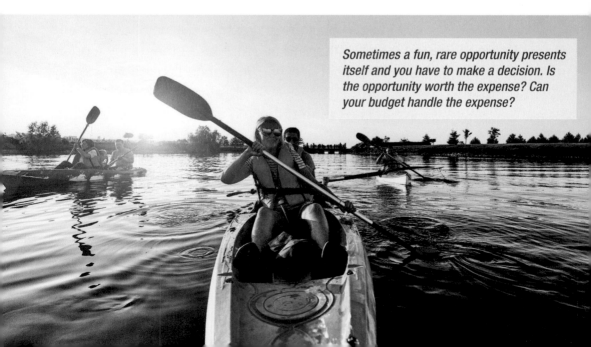

Sometimes a fun, rare opportunity presents itself and you have to make a decision. Is the opportunity worth the expense? Can your budget handle the expense?

Whether you tap into your emergency fund in these situations will be up to you. You will have to decide whether the purchase is worth the risk of not being ready for a more expensive emergency. Ask yourself a few additional questions:

- Is this a unique situation?
- Will I have this opportunity in the future?
- What will happen if I don't take advantage of this now?

A last-minute trip might be a rare opportunity to expand your horizons, deepen a relationship, and enrich your life. It might also be something you and your friend could put off for six months so you have time to save for it. You'll have to decide whether the consequences of not taking the trip outweigh the risk of not being able to pay for another expense if your emergency fund is low. Ask yourself the same questions if a great deal on a car comes along. If a more reliable vehicle will allow you to take a better job in a nearby city, then the purchase might be worth it. Otherwise, you could start a car fund so you're ready when the next deal comes along. A sale on shoes or other clothing is something that will definitely come along again, and could be something you budget for next month.

The Advantage of Being Prepared

When you need to take money out of your emergency fund, look at the money as a loan rather than a gift. Make emergency fund deposits part of your budget until you've reached your goal once again.

Having an emergency fund gives you some control in a difficult situation. Having enough money on hand to take care of the emergency—whether it's a flat tire, broken water heater, or something more serious—can take some of the edge off a challenging situation.

Chapter Six

Bouncing Back

It seemed like a good idea at the time. Lily, age seventeen, thought the marker set she saw on Pinterest would be a great way to enhance her journal. Now the fifty pack of markers sits in her room, barely used. "I've used them like four times," she says. "Maybe I should have waited a little longer to buy them. Now I understand I shouldn't have done that."[37]

Make a Budgeting Mistake?
Welcome to the Club

Lily is far from alone in having regrets over the way she's spent her money. Abbey, age seventeen, admits to spending too much on junk food, and eighteen-year-old Cassidy's mistake was buying too many things and almost draining her account. For Grant, age seventeen, it was a mistake to buy interesting tech at a thrift store, thinking he would sell the items for more than he paid for them. Ryan, age eighteen, spent too much of his savings and then didn't have enough money to get his car repaired. Garrett's poor financial decision was to spend $1,200 on a phone. "It's hard not to spend,"[38] the sixteen-year-old says.

Making the right decisions when it comes to money isn't easy. Mistakes are common, whether that's buying something you don't need or depleting your savings account. It's

It is easy to stop for fast food or fun coffee drinks, but those small purchases add up quickly and can blow your budget.

likely that you'll make a financial misstep at one time or another, and that's nothing to be ashamed of. Mistakes are an opportunity to learn, and the key is to find that lesson and move on.

Owning Up

The first step in overcoming a financial mistake is acknowledging that you've made one. Be honest with yourself. Admitting that you've messed up shows that you're taking responsibility for your actions. This puts you in control, letting you take steps to resolve the situation and learn from what went wrong. Recognizing that you were responsible for the error makes it less likely that you'll make the same mistake again.

You'll probably feel bad about making a mistake, but don't get down on yourself. Spending too much time dwelling on your mistake is a mistake in itself. Instead, think about what you can do so it won't happen again. You can return to good financial habits and make a better decision next time. Cassidy's spending almost depleted her bank account, but she didn't wallow in self-pity. Instead, she reversed course. "I took a reality check and started saving more,"[39] she says.

Remain Calm and Take Action

After you make a financial misstep, you'll need to face the consequences. Don't panic; it's important to keep your cool and deal with what follows. Calmly thinking through the situation can help you come up with a solution.

If you forget to pay a bill or receive an overdue notice, you'll need to come up with a plan for getting the bill paid off. As painful as it might be to address it now, trying to avoid the situation will only make it worse. You might need to ask your parents for a loan or call the company that sent the bill, but setting the bill aside or tossing it in the recycling bin won't make it go away. Be assured that you're far from the first person this has ever happened to. Emily, age seventeen, had to act fast when a payment slipped her mind. "I forgot to pay my car bill," she says. "But then I paid it right away."[40]

> "I took a reality check and started saving more."[39]
>
> —Cassidy, age eighteen

If your bad decision was a purchase you regret, it's possible that you can return the item to the store for the amount you paid for it. Many stores and online sites allow you to return a purchase within a certain time period, such as thirty or sixty days, if the item wasn't used. If you got a paper receipt with your purchase, always save it in a safe spot, just in case you want to return the item. And if the receipt is on your phone, don't delete it until you're certain you're going to keep the item.

Cutting Your Losses

If you're not able to return a purchase and it's something you don't need or don't like, it's possible that you can sell it. The price you get will probably be less than what you paid for it, but something is better than nothing. Rather than feeling bad about the money you lost, you can think of it as payment for some financial education.

Another option would be to donate the item to charity. You wouldn't get money for the item, but giving has its own rewards. You would get the satisfaction of knowing that your purchase is helping someone.

Coming Up with a Plan

After you've come to terms with your mistake, think about what you could do to keep it from happening again. You might want to follow one of these tips:

> **Look in your closet.** Leah, age seventeen, admits she's bought things she really didn't need. "There are five shirts in my closet that still have the tag on them," she says. "I have hair and skin products I thought I needed but I've used like once." Now when she sees something that catches her eye, she thinks about what she already owns. "I think of other products that I have that do the same thing, they're just different brands,"[41] she says.

> **Change your routine.** If you're spending too much money on fast food, try to avoid going past your favorite restaurants on your way home from school or work. Switching your route can help you avoid the temptation to stop in.

> **Do some research.** When you're making a purchase, read about the product. Talk to others who have owned it to see what they've learned. This will help you get an idea of how much you can expect to pay and how long it will last. If it's a big purchase like a computer or car, some research can help you understand the cost of upkeep and repairs.

> **Learn more.** It's a good habit to keep learning about money, whether that's in financial management classes or by reading blogs and books. Additional knowledge will give

you a firm foundation for financial decisions and will help you say no when you need to. In addition, it will help you continue to make informed decisions as your financial situation changes when you get a full-time job and move out on your own.

Friends and Finance

Learning more about money and finance can also help you understand when you need to say no and give you the strength to do it. As you look at where your money is going, you might become aware that you're spending money in an effort to keep up with your friends. If you hang out with a group that buys expensive clothes or jewelry, has the latest technology, or is always eating out, you might feel like you're expected to do the

Need a Car? Do Your Research

A car is an expensive purchase, and when you're looking to buy one, there may be come costs you didn't consider. Sara, age eighteen, wishes she had set more money aside before buying a car. "I didn't save enough when I bought my car and my savings hurt for a little while," she says.

When you buy a car, remember that you'll also need to pay for the following:

- insurance
- registration and license fees
- gas
- oil changes
- repairs

To save money, consider buying a used car rather than one that's new. Used cars cost less, and you might be able to save enough to buy one for cash rather than making monthly payments.

Quoted in author questionnaire, "Building a Budget and Saving Money Survey," Survey, March 16, 2020.

same. As great as it is to have friends, sometimes they can lead you in the wrong financial direction. Financial counselor Becky Smith has seen it happen. "People influence how you spend your money," she says. "Your friend is going to want you to go to the movies."[42]

It can be tough to tell your friends that an expense just isn't in your budget right now. Rachel, age twenty-six, wasn't excited about going on a vacation with friends, but when they asked her to go along, she couldn't bring herself to turn them down. She found that the trip wasn't well planned, in addition to being costly,

Oftentimes we find ourselves spending money to keep up with our friends. It is important to know your limits and when you have to say no to spending.

and she regretted her lack of resolve. "If you're going to invest in a vacation, make sure it's something you want to spend money on," she says. "There's nothing worse than wasting time trying to figure out what to do when you could be enjoying your vacation."[43]

A romantic relationship might also lead you down the wrong path. Falling in love with someone who constantly wants you to buy things for him or her can leave you broke and feeling used. The lesson? Learn to say no. A boyfriend or girlfriend who disappears after you stop spending money on him or her isn't worth hanging around with.

If you feel like your circle of friends has been doing things that cost too much money lately, talk it over with them. They might feel the same way you do. Lauren, age seventeen, likes to eat out with her friends, but sometimes the group agrees that they need to take a break. "If we've all been eating out together a lot we will just eat at home and then do something,"[44] she says.

> "We've all made mistakes. Yes, you can overcome them."[45]
>
> —Becky Smith, financial counselor

A Silver Lining

Spending too much on fast food or buying a shirt that you never wear can turn out to be a good experience if it teaches you the value of learning to manage your money more diligently. A spending mistake could inspire you to do a better job of tracking your expenses, start an emergency fund, and stick to your spending plan. "We've all made mistakes," Smith notes. "Yes, you can overcome them."[45]

It's not uncommon to adjust and revise a budget. Making changes is part of the budgeting process. Smith describes the budgeting process as a circle rather than a straight line: you create a budget, put it into practice, see how you did, and budget again. "You budget, try, and learn," Smith says. "Some people say budgets don't work, but they only go around the circle once. They put numbers on paper and found they couldn't live by those numbers, so therefore budgets don't work. If it doesn't work perfectly the first time, no kidding! It takes a while."[46]

By paying attention to your mistakes and working to correct them, you'll learn lessons that help you do a better job of tracking spending, saving for emergencies, and sticking to your budget throughout your life. Logan found that his spending habits improved while he was in high school. He wasn't especially careful with money as a freshman and sophomore, even though he knew he should take spending seriously. He became more

Life Lesson

Kyle, age twenty-eight, wasn't a huge fan of saving and budgeting until he found himself without a steady income. He had been teaching English at a school in Vietnam but couldn't pass up an opportunity to move to Indonesia. He didn't have a job waiting for him there, but he figured he would pick something up. "My mistake was being overconfident about the amount of money I had, and not thinking my savings would run low. I was overly optimistic," he says. "This made me realize just how important the stability of using money wisely is."

After moving back to the United States, he found a job as a content writer. He began building his savings by cutting expenses. He rented an inexpensive apartment with a friend to split the cost of rent and utilities, rarely eats out, and uses public transportation rather than owning a car. He buys cell phone minutes for texting and talking only and has a used iPod he uses for social media. He doesn't take vacations until he's saved enough money to pay for them. By watching his expenses, he is able to set aside money for retirement and regularly puts money into a savings account and emergency fund. "Now that I have more saved I've realized it takes a big burden off," he says. "I feel like I could lose my job and I would be OK for a while. It feels good to have some savings."

Kyle, interview by the author, July 12, 2020.

aware of his spending during his junior and senior years, setting aside fifteen dollars for bowling on the weekends, being careful with money spent on eating out, and putting off larger purchases such as a new cell phone. It became common sense to save and not go overboard on spending. At seventeen, he's already learned some important financial lessons. "I'm conscious about what I spend my money on," he says. "You should use it for things you want to use it for, but always be sure to make sure of yourself first. Make sure you're in a good financial place to stay afloat and are able to pay bills on time."[47]

"I'm conscious about what I spend my money on."[47]

—Logan, age seventeen

Source Notes

Introduction: The Freedom of Budgeting

1. Becky Smith, interview by the author, March 28, 2020.
2. Smith, interview.
3. Smith, interview.

Chapter One: Where Do I Start?

4. Smith, interview.
5. Quoted in author questionnaire, "Building a Budget and Saving Money Survey," Survey, March 16, 2020.
6. Smith, interview.
7. Logan, interview by the author, July 13, 2020.
8. Quoted in author questionnaire, "Building a Budget and Saving Money Survey."
9. Quoted in Gillian B. White, "Getting to the Bottom of Americans' Fascination with Wealth," *The Atlantic,* May 16, 2017. www.theatlantic.com.

Chapter Two: Building a Budget

10. Rachel, interview by the author, July 10, 2020.
11. Eric, interview by the author, May 11, 2020.
12. Smith, interview.
13. Quoted in author questionnaire, "Building a Budget and Saving Money Survey."
14. Eric, interview.

Chapter Three: Realistic Expectations and Long-Term Goals

15. Lauren, interview by the author, June 19, 2020.
16. Leah, interview by the author, June 19, 2020.
17. Laura Finaldi, "Coronavirus Florida: Stress Causing Some to Impulse Shop," *Sarasota (FL) Herald-Tribune*, April 27, 2020. www.heraldtribune.com.

18. Kyle, interview by the author, July 12, 2020.
19. Leah, interview.
20. Kelly, interview by the author, May 17, 2020.
21. Red, interview by the author, July 13, 2020.
22. Emma, interview by the author, July 2, 2020.
23. Lily, interview by the author, June 19, 2020.
24. Lily, interview.
25. Quoted in author questionnaire, "Building a Budget and Saving Money Survey."

Chapter Four: How to Find the Sweet Spot

26. Nick, interview by the author, June 19, 2020.
27. Quoted in Joe Pinsker, "The Reason Many Ultrarich People Aren't Satisfied with Their Wealth," *The Atlantic*, December 4, 2018. www.theatlantic.com.
28. Emma, interview.
29. Quoted in Sarah Jane Gilbert, "Spending on Happiness," Harvard Business School, June 2, 2008. https://hbswk.hbs.edu.
30. Leah, interview by the author, June 19, 2020.

Chapter Five: The Unexpected: Be Ready for an Emergency

31. Leah, interview.
32. Quoted in author questionnaire, "Building a Budget and Saving Money Survey."
33. Lauren, interview.
34. Emily, interview by the author, July 10, 2020.
35. Smith, interview.
36. Smith, interview.

Chapter Six: Bouncing Back

37. Lily, interview.
38. Quoted in author questionnaire, "Building a Budget and Saving Money Survey."
39. Quoted in author questionnaire, "Building a Budget and Saving Money Survey."

40. Quoted in author questionnaire, "Building a Budget and Saving Money Survey."
41. Leah, interview.
42. Smith, interview.
43. Rachel, interview.
44. Lauren, interview.
45. Smith, interview.
46. Smith, interview.
47. Logan, interview by the author, May 6, 2020.

For Further Research

Books

Craig E. Blohm, *Managing Money*. San Diego, CA:Reference-Point Press, 2019.

Michele Cagan, *Budgeting 101: From Getting Out of Debt and Tracking Expenses to Setting Financial Goals and Building Your Savings, Your Essential Guide to Budgeting*. Avon, MA: Adams Media, 2018.

Michele Cagan, *The Infographic guide to personal finance: a visual reference for everything you need to know.* New York: Adams Media, 2017.

Chelsea Fagan, *The Financial Diet: A Total Beginner's Guide to Getting Good with Money.* New York: Henry Holt, 2018.

Tina Hay, *Napkin Finance: Build Your Wealth in 30 Seconds or Less.* New York: Dey Street, 2019.

Jill Schlesinger, *The Dumb Things Smart People Do with Their Money*. New York: Ballantine, 2019.

Internet Sources

Johan Almenberg et al., "Attitudes Toward Debt and Debt Behavior," National Bureau of Economic Research, 2018. www.nber.org.

Consumer Financial Protection Bureau, "CFPB Financial Well-Being Scale." https://files.consumerfinance.gov.

Denise Fournier, "From Impulsive to Intentional," *Mindfully Present, Fully Alive* (blog), *Psychology Today*, August 1, 2017. www.psychologytoday.com.

Catherine S. Harvey, "Unlocking the Potential of Emergency Savings Accounts," AARP, 2019. www.aarp.org.

Sarah O'Brien, "Consumers Cough Up $5,400 a Year on Impulse Purchases," CNBC, February 23, 2018. www.cnbc.com.

Joe Pinsker, "The Reason Many Ultrarich People Aren't Satisfied with Their Wealth," *The Atlantic*, December 4, 2018. www.theatlantic.com.

John Rampton, "Science Says Money Does Buy Happiness If You Spend It the Right Way," *Entrepreneur,* March 2, 2018, www.entrepreneur.com.

Gillian B. White, "Getting to the Bottom of Americans' Fascination with Wealth," *The Atlantic*, May 16, 2017. www.theatlantic.com.

Websites

Consumer Finance, Federal Trade Commission (www.ftc.gov /news-events/media-resources/consumer-finance). The Federal Trade Commission is a government agency that works to stop scams and help consumers protect their money. This webpage contains links to information about credit cards, payday lending, financial technology, and debt relief and credit repair scams, among other topics.

Consumer Financial Protection Bureau (www.consumerfinance.gov). This website contains information on managing finances. It offers consumer tools on topics such as auto loans, bank accounts, credit reports, and student loans. It also provides financial decision guides and personal stories about financial decisions. In addition, the website features a section called Ask CFPB, which offers answers to hundreds of financial questions.

MyMoney.gov (www.mymoney.gov). This website from the Financial Literacy & Education Commission provides basic information about financial concepts, including earning, borrowing, and saving.

360 Degrees of Financial Literacy (www.360financialliteracy. org). The American Institute of CPAs offers information on topics such as credit and debt, taxes, and spending and saving on this website. It also offers dozens of calculators that show how savings add up.

Index

Picture Credits

Cover: Eskaylim/iStock

5: shironosov/iStock
9: Halfpoint/iStock
10: pixiedeluxe/iStock
12: FatCamera/iStock
17: MediaProduction/iStock
26: FatCamera/iStock
30: william87 /iStock
33: Topalov/iStock
39: BongkamThanyakij/iStock
43: LightFieldStudios/iStock
46: elinedesignservices/iStock
51: monkeybusinessimages/iStock
54: Sezeryadigar/iStock
59: 6okean/iStock
62: frantic00/iStock
66: MartinDimitrov/iStock

About the Author

Terri Dougherty has written dozens of books for young adults and children. She lives in Appleton, Wisconsin, with her husband. They have three grown children who are learning more about budgeting every day. Terri loves picking up and passing on new tips about how to save money.